THE STORY OF THE NATIVITY

Text by Elena Pasquali
Illustrations copyright © 2014 Sophie Windham
This edition copyright © 2014 Lion Hudson

Published by Lion Children's Books
an imprint of
Lion Hudson plc
Wilkinson House, Jordan Hill Road,
Oxford OX2 8DR, England
www.lionhudson.com/lionchildrens

ISBN 978 0 7459 6541 3

First edition 2014

A catalogue record for this book is available
from the British Library

Printed and bound in China, June 2014, LH06

THE STORY OF THE
NATIVITY

Retold by Elena Pasquali ✸ Illustrated by Sophie Windham

LION
CHILDREN'S

I n the little town of Nazareth, Mary was dreaming of her wedding. "It seems that I've been looking forward to the day for so long," she said.

In his workshop, Joseph smiled.

"My family is proud of its past – being descended from King David. But soon Mary will be my wife and we can be proud of our future. It is all turning out just as I hoped."

Then God sent the angel Gabriel to Nazareth, and to Mary.

"Peace be with you," said the angel. "God has chosen you to be the mother of a baby boy: Jesus.

"He will be known as God's Son; he will be God's chosen king – greater than King David of ancient times – and his kingdom will never end."

Mary listened in awe.

"How can I be a mother? I'm not even married yet!" she said.

"All this can happen because of God," replied the angel.

"Then may what you have said come true," said Mary.

When Joseph heard that Mary was expecting a baby, he was dismayed.
An angel spoke to him in a dream. "Take Mary as your wife," said the
angel. "Her child is God's Son. Through him, God will bless the world."

Joseph awoke in good heart regarding his marriage... only to hear news that made everyone downhearted.

"Everyone must go to their home town to register as taxpayers, by order of the emperor."

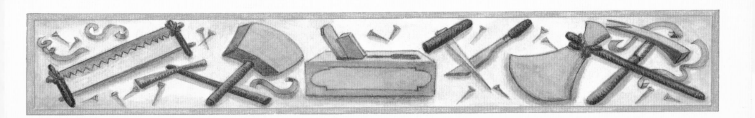

Joseph made a plan.

He hurried to find Mary. "We will go together to my home town," he told her. "Bethlehem, where King David was born hundreds of years ago.

"There, we will register as a family."

It was all agreed. Amid great excitement, Mary and Joseph set out together.

They were not the only ones making a journey to register their names.
When Mary and Joseph reached Bethlehem, the town was crowded.
There was no more room for guests.

The only place they found to shelter was where an ox munched and a
donkey stamped and shuffled. There, in the night, Mary's baby was born.
She wrapped the infant in swaddling clothes and laid him in a manger.

On the hillsides that sloped away from the town, shepherds were awake, taking care of their flocks. Alert for danger... thieves, perhaps, or wild animals.

An angel appeared. "Good news," cried the angel. "Joy to all the world.

"Tonight, in King David's city, your saviour has been born. A new king: God's chosen king.

"Go to Bethlehem! See for yourselves! The child is wrapped in swaddling clothes and cradled in a manger."

All at once the night-time world was bright. A thousand thousand angels, all singing.

"Glory to God in highest heaven.

"Peace on earth to those with whom he is pleased."

As swiftly as they had come, the angels vanished into heaven.

Awestruck and astonished, the shepherds left their sheep. They hurried to Bethlehem, and searched the darkened streets until they came to the stable.

There, in the lamplight, were Joseph and Mary and a newborn child,
just as the angel had said.

Mary listened wide-eyed to their story, treasuring every word.

In nearby Jerusalem, Herod ruled the land on behalf of the emperor. When foreigners came to the city with troubling news, he demanded to see them.

"You say a star has led you here," he said. "You say it is the sign that a king has been born to my people, even though I am the appointed ruler."

He leaned closer. "My advisors tell me that, one day, God's chosen king will be born in Bethlehem.

"Go – see if you can find the child. If you do, come and tell me." He furrowed his brow. "I will need to go and worship too."

The foreigners set out.

There was the star they had followed for so many miles, shining on the road to Bethlehem and finally stopping low over one particular house.

They went inside and found Mary, and her baby son.
"The newborn king," they exclaimed. "We have come to worship him."
Respectfully they brought out their gifts: gold, frankincense, and myrrh.

"We will not go and tell Herod about the child," they agreed. "Did we not hear an angel warning us in our dreams?"

"That man fears a rival."

"He will seek to harm him."

An angel also spoke to Joseph.

"Hurry. King Herod has heard rumours of a newborn king and will be looking for the child. Take Mary and Jesus to Egypt and stay there until it is safe."

Jesus was no longer a baby when the time came for Mary and Joseph
to return to Nazareth. There, he grew up with the other children,
every year taller, every year wiser.

"Such a good son," everyone said. "What a blessing to his family."

Only heaven knew how soon Jesus would bring a greater blessing
to all the world.

Other titles from Lion Children's Books

The Child of Christmas *Sophie Piper & Sophy Williams*
The Shepherd Girl of Bethlehem *Carey Morning & Alan Marks*
The Story of Christmas *Mary Joslin & Alida Massari*
The Three Trees *Elena Pasquali & Sophie Windham*